tap that!

TYFFANY HOWARD, JD

BALBOA.
PRESS

A DIVISION OF HAY HOUSE

Balboa Press books may be ordered through booksellers or by contacting:

Balboa Press
A Division of Hay House
1663 Liberty Drive
Bloomington, IN 47403
www.balboapress.com
1 (877) 407-4847

Printed in the United States of America.

ISBN: 978-1-4525-9351-7 (sc)
ISBN: 978-1-4525-9350-0 (e)

Library of Congress Control Number: 2014903595

Balboa Press rev. date: 3/17/2014

For my greatest teachers:
Mama, Anthony, K.Y., and Catherine

Contents

Welcome ix

Operator's Instructions xvii

Chapter 1   What the Hell Is Tapping? 1

Chapter 2   "Let's Get It On" 14

Chapter 3   Why You Trippin'? 22

Chapter 4   You're All That and a Bag of Chips 29

Chapter 5   "You Told Harpo to Beat Me?" 36

Chapter 6   We Have Come This Far by Faith 43

Chapter 7   Give Me Some of That Sweet Potato Pie 50

Chapter 8   Mo' Money, Mo' Money 55

We Out 63

Acknowledgments 67

Check This Out 71

This Is How I Roll 73

Welcome

Every Sunday in any church or place of worship, especially an African American church, someone begins the Sunday morning service by welcoming those who have come to worship. I know this very well. When I was a little girl, I was a member of Rehobeth Primitive Baptist Church in Austin, Texas. My granddaddy was a preacher, so as the oldest grandchild of a preacher, I had certain responsibilities. Along with singing in the choir and being an usher, I was occasionally asked to give the welcome. One Sunday, when I was not more than seven or eight years old, I nervously walked to the front of the church in my little dress and ponytails and said, "You are welcome to sing, pray, and shout. You are welcome." It was simple, but the congregation responded with a loving amen. It was fun being a kid and getting the support needed to grow confidence in myself. The African proverb "It takes a village to raise a child," from my experience, is true. More than that, I believe with all my heart that it takes each of us working together to grow a world filled with light. Yes, I am my brother and sister's keeper.

That leads me to what brought about this book. Today is Saturday, February 16, 2013. I am sitting in my apartment in Temple, Texas, inspired by the light of the world. For the past ten days, I have participated in the Fifth Annual Tapping World Summit. Nick Ortner, author of *The Tapping Solution*, is the producer of the summit. However, he is not the first to introduce me to tapping. From August 4–7, 2012, I participated in the Tao Life Practice training at the Sedona Mago Retreat in Cottonwood, Arizona. The retreat is a stone's throw from Sedona, Arizona. At this retreat, I learned meridian tapping as a way to heal emotional and physical trauma imprinted on my cellular memory. Meridian tapping, tapping, or Gary Craig's EFT (Emotional Freedom Techniques) are pretty much all the same. Throughout this book, I will just call it tapping. So what is tapping? I will get to that soon.

I would like to thank all the teachers at the Sedona Mago Retreat. I went there because I felt like I wanted to die. I knew I needed help, and I believe in self-help. I live by natural, medicine-free, doctor-free healing methods. I find it interesting that I am writing this book almost one year after my divorce. Allow me to elaborate. Monday, February 11, 2013, would have been my ninth wedding anniversary, and last year, on February 29, 2012, my husband and I got divorced. Two months later, my girlfriend and I broke up, and it devastated me. Yes, that is right, my girlfriend. I am alternative. If you haven't caught on yet, it means that I am attracted to men and women. Back to why I wanted to die. For eight years, I dealt with shame, guilt, self-loathing, and heartbreak.

My ex-husband was aware of my challenges. At times, the effect of being in the closet and dealing with my own religious and personal beliefs about loving men and women made me physically ill. I would get so sick that my ex-husband told me I should have a sexual experience with a woman to find out if that was what I really wanted. Sadly, he probably wishes that he had never suggested or allowed such an experience. Although a selfless and loving gesture in the beginning, in the end, he was not pleased. For his sacrifice and support of my well-being, I will always love my ex-husband and be forever grateful to him. So when she kissed me that Friday night while we sat on the floor of her living room watching a movie, thus began what I thought would be a love that would last a lifetime.

The woman with whom I fell in love, Catherine, was my best friend and business partner. I knew we had a connection that was beyond this lifetime. When it ended, I realized that the purpose of our relationship was to help me heal some lingering daddy abandonment issues. So I was forced to swim in my sea of abandonment, unworthiness, trust, and self-love. The pain of living life without her was so unbearable that I wanted to die. I didn't understand why we couldn't be together. She made the choice to stay where she was, and that was not with me. My heart was like, "Ouch!" And my crazy mind kept playing our time together over and over, causing me to question why I was learning this particular lesson. I didn't know it at the time, but I was being given an opportunity to grow. At night I would curl up in a little ball in my bed and beg God to help me. I would say, "Please, God, I can't take this pain. Help me!" Because I know God helps those who help themselves. I was committed to healing my emotional wounds. So I searched the web for spiritual retreats and found the Sedona Mago Retreat.

At the retreat, I learned that humans have three bodies: physical, spiritual, and energy. In the past, I would deal with pain by closing my heart, putting up a huge wall, and withdrawing emotionally to protect myself. This caused a numbing feeling. I learned at Sedona Mago Retreat that my spiritual body had separated from my physical body, creating a feeling of numbness and emptiness. Wow! I learned that I had to reconnect those bodies. With the help of the instructors at Sedona Mago Retreat, I did. They saved my life and taught me how to eat, sleep, walk, breathe, and live in gratitude for life, loving God, loving all beings, and especially loving myself.

So I went to the Sedona Mago Retreat to work on me and learn how to heal my emotional wounds. One of the healing tools I learned was tapping. The folks at the retreat called it meridian tapping, and Gary Craig developed a method called EFT (Emotional Freedom Techniques). I just call it tapping. I have found tapping to be so useful in lessening my anxiety, fear, anger, and stress that I thought African Americans and people of color should know about it. Why have I centered this book on African Americans and others who share our experiences? Because I don't find this information in our community. And I was reared to believe in "each one, teach one." African Americans have countless emotional and physical wounds associated with slavery, discrimination, unemployment, self-hatred, unworthiness, abandonment, poverty, racism, etc. We need to question and stop the cycle of poor environmental conditioning.

That conditioning falsely tells us that we are our race, our skin color, our clothes, our bodies, our past, our job, our sexuality, our mistakes, our weight, our car, our neighborhood, and on and on. We are none of those things. We are divine souls of light within a human body. Knowing that, I am saddened when I see the many people walking around with glazed-over eyes. You've heard the term "the walking dead." I see this dis-ease everywhere I go. Seeing people wearing masks and living unfulfilled breaks my heart. I am no stranger to the emptiness I see because I have been there myself. So I asked this question of myself: "Tyffany, how can you know something and not share it?" I had my doubts about sharing this information. Why? Blacks can be hard on each other, and I would have to face some of my core beliefs like "success is dangerous" and "I am not valuable" and "I am not enough." I remember being called "Oreo" and "white girl" in high school by other black kids. Those comments really hurt. But I know that it wasn't really about me. Anyway, I trust God, and I know that I was meant to write this book. Just so you know, this book will discuss issues that may cause some to feel uncomfortable. If that happens, maybe you will see your response as an opportunity to grow. Healing is feeling uncomfortable and being stretched to the point that you feel uneasy. God told me to write this book, and as I wrote each word and every chapter, I asked God to assist and guide me. I could not sit on the sidelines, watch people suffer, and do nothing to help. The truth is that we are all connected, so when you suffer, I suffer.

Like most African Americans, I grew up in the church. My dad's family is Primitive Baptist, and my mom is a black Muslim. Being exposed to both Christianity and Islam was a real education for me. When I went to college, I studied Judaism, and later in life I practiced Buddhism. After all those diverse teachings, I now know that I have a direct connection to God so I don't have to blindly search for a relationship with him through religion. I can talk to God myself and get answers. Some may say that I am spiritual. The mind wants to put something in a box, so it gives it a label. I describe it as having a relationship with God. I digressed a little. The point is that most black folks go to church every Sunday and maybe a couple of days during the week. That being said, stand up if you are happy and abundant, your work is joyous, you are healthy, you are stress free, you have let go of the past, you forgive white folks, you have stopped hating yourself and other blacks and gays, and you love and accept yourself. If you did not stand up, ask yourself if you may need other healing techniques to complement your religious practice. You will feel so much better, and your life will unfold in such grand ways. Can I get a witness?

No, I am not a medical doctor, psychologist, therapist, psychiatrist, or an acupuncturist. I am a healer of a different sort. I make no promises about any individual's particular result. My intention is to introduce African Americans and people of color to a technique that has been proven to reduce emotional and physical pain. Healing is not just for those who can afford it—it is for all of us. So I decided that if this knowledge is not being shared in the communities of color, I had to share it. I have to repay humanity and the earth for my blessings, so this book is one way of saying I am grateful for all that I have been given. Know that this little book is not an extensive manual, but it is enough to get you started tapping. I am not a tapping guru or expert, but my skill level is enough to introduce you to tapping. If you want more information about tapping or Gary Craig's EFT, please look at my resource section titled "Check This Out" at the end of this book. I intend *tap that!* to be the seed and the catalyst for spiritual exploration and personal growth. Once the seed is planted, you have to water and nurture it.

So if you haven't figured it out yet, this book is about tapping. A good preacher would say, "On our program for this Sunday morning, we have tapping—tapping for better relationships, tapping for less stress, tapping in our beauty, tapping down fear, tapping in our greatness, tapping off that weight, and tapping in more money; we are going to tap this and *tap that!* Can I get an amen?

Operator's Instructions

Before you begin this new adventure, you are going to need to get a few things. What do you need? Get a journal, notebook, or any kind of paper to keep a record of your progress. When you begin to tap, you will measure the intensity level of what you are feeling from zero to ten. After a round of tapping, you will again measure the level of intensity. That's why you need paper to keep a record of your measurements. If you don't write down where you are, how will you know how far you have gone? I don't want to hear "this tapping hasn't done anything for me." I know my people. Next, find a nice comfortable place to tap. Just so you know, I tap anywhere—courthouse, car, airport, plane, bathroom, etc. You decide where you would like to tap. Then ask yourself, "What is bothering me now?" We are all experiencing the human condition. That is, all the everyday stuff we deal with in these human bodies—work, stress, sadness, guilt, resentment, physical pain, anger, etc. The list doesn't end. I practice being aware of what arises in my body and mind. So if I am out somewhere and someone gives me a dirty look, whatever my mind thinks, my body will feel. That is when I tap. I might remember a situation from my past and get angry. That is when I tap. There are no rules that govern when to tap or when not to tap. You are the decision maker; however, I strongly suggest that you tap daily for at least five minutes. Sometimes I turn on some inspirational or soothing music as I tap. To be honest, I haven't seen or heard any EFT practitioner suggest or not suggest the use of music. Music is so much a part of African American culture that it seems natural to me to incorporate music with tapping. I don't know whether the music affects the benefits of tapping or not. When I tap on my sadness and hear "Somebody Bigger" from *The Preacher's Wife* soundtrack, my soul is uplifted. So for me, music soothes my soul, and the tapping seems to flow like the spoken word at a poetry slam. Tapping is more than just speaking your truth about how you feel; it is an art form. And if music is used as a complement to yoga, meditation, and Reiki sessions, then why not tapping? Again, it is your decision whether or not to use music. The goal is to get you excited about tapping. Once you have a sheet of paper, something to write with, a glass of water, a place to tap, and a problem to tap about, grab a good attitude and an open mind. Like a kid on the first day of school, you have all the supplies you need to get you off to a great first day of tapping. Are you ready to learn more?

Chapter 1

What the Hell Is Tapping?

You may have been tapped. You may have been the one doing the tapping. But, you have never been tapped like this. Tapping is using your fingertips to tap on your body as you speak the truth about how you feel regarding an event, physical illness, money matters, or anything that signals fear or pain to your brain. The continued development of tapping can be attributed to the work of chiropractor George Goodhart, psychiatrist John Diamond, Dr. Roger Callahan, Gary Craig, and Dr. Patricia Carrington. As mentioned earlier, in the tapping world, you may hear it referred to as meridian tapping, tapping, or EFT (Emotional Freedom Techniques). The founder of EFT is Gary Craig. Throughout this guidebook, I will use the term tapping unless I refer to one of Gary Craig's specific techniques.

While EFT uses negative language while tapping, sometimes I am guided by spirit to use positive talk when I process a negative emotional memory. For instance, rather than tap on being worried because I don't have enough money, I may tap on how grateful I am for what I already have and that I am open to all the ways that more money will come to me. Once you learn how to tap and feel comfortable, you decide how you wish to process your emotions.

With tapping, there are no needles, pills, or surgery. Tapping is as simple as thinking of an emotional memory, event, or problem and using your fingers to tap on various endpoints on your body's meridian lines. There are twelve major meridians which are the basis of ancient Chinese acupuncture. Meridians are defined as energy channels or currents that carry the vital life force energy to particular organs of the body. Each meridian also has what's called an "endpoint," a specific location on the surface of the body where you can access the energy channel. This point can be manipulated using acupuncture needles or simple touch (acupressure) to balance or unlock the energy flow through that particular meridian.[1]

Although tapping is not a substitute for traditional medical care, it can be applied in addition to utilizing western medicine. There is little or no pain. The application is so simple that professionals, such as therapists, teachers, physicians, sports coaches, massage therapists, chiropractors, acupuncturists, homeopaths, and spiritual life coaches are learning tapping to apply to the people they serve in their respective professions. Even parents are learning how to tap to use on their children. Depending on the severity of the emotional experience or situation, you may cry as you remember the event. Remember that tapping should not be applied to people with serious psychological problems unless you have the appropriate training. This is not a game, so please be responsible with this tool.

Why Tap?

How many of you get up to go to church every Sunday morning, and after all the praying, singing, and preaching, you still feel depressed, angry, sad, and miserable? My granddaddy, the late Reverend R. H. Howard, could preach like nobody's business. I have fond memories of witnessing his performance, but when all the shouting was over, I would look into people's faces and still see emptiness. The effects of Sunday morning service wore off quickly. Black people still had to deal with the week ahead, that is, operating in a system that we don't seem to be able to integrate into well.

I know what you want to ask me: "I am black, living in America, so how can tapping help me?" Tapping will help you to process, in a healing way, those issues that can keep you stuck, unhealthy, angry and unemployed. We have been through a lot of trauma in this country. The trauma experienced by our ancestors has been imprinted on our DNA. In addition, the daily trauma that we experience by virtue of living in this country causes stress. In our community, stress wipes us out! However, at some point, it is time to stop reliving the trauma, stop resenting white folks, stop the self-hatred, stop the hatred of each other, stop using food that is not healthy for you to self-medicate, stop the destruction of the black family, and stop living in lack by hanging on to limiting beliefs.

At some point, I realized that hanging on to other people's stuff was not healthy for me. You must realize that you can't change how people treat you or feel about you. You can do something about how you react to other people's ugliness. Hanging on to what somebody did in the past or is doing to you now does not hurt the other person; it hurts you. We have to rewire our environmental conditioning, that is, those beliefs that we learned from our family, teachers, friends, and society that are false and no longer serve us.

For me, it is about quality of life. I wanted to be free of the killer we call *stress*. I wanted to forgive and live in the present. I wanted to be abundant and happy. Why was I stressed? Even though I did everything mainstream America said I had to do to succeed (e.g., go to college, get a job, get married, buy a house and a nice car, so on and so forth), I still had to deal with racism, resentment of the system, anger, limiting beliefs about money and who I could love, etc. So again, why was I still stressed after accomplishing the so-called American dream? I will tell you.

I have discussed this theory with my ex-husband many times, and I have accepted it as truth. I will discuss it in depth later, but I will throw it out there so you can chew on it as you read this book. We, black folks, experience so much stress even when we are successful as defined by the mainstream, because we cannot fully integrate into this Western system. Simply, we are stressed out, angry, resentful, unhealthy, and experience lack because we don't accept who we are; we fail at the attempts to change who we are to fit into this Western system. You are trying to meet a standard that you will never be able to meet.

Yes, we are all connected to each other and the Divine Spirit, God, Allah, Ja, and all the other names humans give the higher intelligence. And yes, all higher selves are identical and indistinguishable; however, in these human bodies our experiences on planet Earth are beautifully different. I want to be clear. The trees and the ocean are both life and have qualities unique to their life form. But we don't ask the tree to become the ocean in order to accept it. We accept that the tree is a tree and the ocean is the ocean. The standard makers in mainstream America demand that we, the tree, become the ocean. That, my brothers and sisters, is illogical and physically impossible.

But, like children, black folks still seek the approval of their parents, white folks, and try and try to become the ocean. How silly! You cannot reach the mountaintop if you are weighed down by too much baggage. I have experienced poverty, racism, and sexism. I have been called the *n* word on the golf course and by court-appointed clients who didn't want me to represent them. I have had to hide who I am and dim my light all my life because I was afraid that others would harm me if I didn't. Dr. Martin Luther King Jr., Malcolm X, Angela Davis, the Dalai Lama, and Jesus had the courage to shine their lights. So I have no excuse, and neither do you. We have to stop living in the past and future. The present is where miracles happen. God wants you to be happy, healthy, and prosperous. And you know that God helps those who help themselves. It boils down to what you believe you deserve and whether or not you want to live the life that God intended for you to live.

That pain, resentment, anger, fear, feeling of unworthiness, feelings of being unloved, and feelings of "I don't have enough" can be eased if not healed. Your stress can be relieved. You have to ask yourself if you want to heal or stay where you are. I have already answered that question for myself. Tapping can be applied to rewire your brain. Your brain stores every memory, including memories related to negative experiences. This is how the brain works. Here are two examples that you will understand. In these two situations, your brain will send a signal that screams, "fear and danger": (1) you meet someone you like and you don't know if that person likes you too, or (2) you have a bill due and you don't have the money to pay it.

The brain was designed by evolution to protect us from physical danger like being eaten by a lion. And the brain can't distinguish between a physical danger, like being eaten by a lion, and an emotional danger, like rejection or fear of having your lights turned off. So if you have experienced rejection and a new person comes along, the brain remembers that feeling of rejection and sends a message that could translate into you sweating because of fear, anxiety, anger, or some other emotion or physical reaction.

By tapping on the meridian endpoints and speaking the truth about how you feel about a certain experience, you rewire the brain to feel safe and calm, thereby allowing energy to flow. You ask, what energy? Humans, like trees, the ocean, the sky, a bird, and all living things, have life force energy, also known as *chi* or *prana,* that flows throughout our body. When it is blocked, we get sick, we gain weight, we get stressed, and we don't make any money. The goal is to unblock that energy so it is balanced and harmonized and flows.

I know some of you are skeptical. I wasn't skeptical at all. When I was introduced to meridian tapping at the

Sedona Mago Retreat, I didn't question it. I just did it. And after doing it, I knew it was worth shouting about. My spirit was grateful. Let me tell you something. You won't learn about tapping in the black churches. No one is telling you these things. No one is coming into our community and saying, "Hey, here's something to relieve some of your suffering." Most times I feel that as a group we are falling farther behind. I know some of you are thinking that I don't know what I am talking about, when I say "behind."

A black man is president. Ask yourself, "How has the fact that President Barak Obama is biracial, helped me?" I know you are proud. Are you healthier? Are you making more money? Are you happy? Are you in a loving relationship? Are you feeling better about being in your black body in America? Have you stopped blaming white people for everything bad that happens to you? Many black people are struck somewhere in the past and don't want to budge. You can't evolve in this world if you don't have the tools. Most of our community is not ready for this new age of consciousness. So what are you going to do? If you truly want to be free, you must let go of that emotional baggage. You let go of it by processing your emotional memories in a healthy way. How? Tapping.

How to Tap

The procedures described in this step-by-step format should be clear and easy to follow. If not, it is my first book, so don't be too hard on me.

Step 1:
Focus on the discomfort or problem. The discomfort can be physical like neck pain or a craving for food. It can also be emotional like fear, anger, anxiety, or limiting beliefs, etc.

Step 2:
Measure the level of discomfort or how much it upsets you on a scale of 0 to 10. Zero represents no discomfort, and 10 represents extreme discomfort. Don't worry or get distracted about selecting a specific number. The key is to get started, so just give yourself a number and move on. This is when you use your journal, notebook, or any sheet of paper to record the level of intensity. Why do you need to measure and write it down? After you tap, you will remeasure to determine whether there has been any change in your level of intensity. And I know you guys. Some of you will say, "Tapping didn't do anything for me." That's why I want you to record the before-tapping level of intensity and the after-tapping level of intensity.

Step 3:
Gary Craig's EFT uses a setup phrase. The current setup phrase is "Even though I have this _____(name the issue), I deeply and completely accept myself."[2] I prefer to use this setup phrase: "Even though I have this_____ (name of issue), I deeply and completely love and accept myself." Or you can use customized language. Check out this example: "Even though I have this pain in my neck, I deeply and completely love and accept myself." Recite

the setup statement three times as you tap on the karate chop point. The description and illustration of the karate chop point is on the following pages.

Step 4:
Repeat the problem in one word or a short phrase while tapping on the other eight points. From the example in step 3, the problem to repeat is *this pain* or *this pain in my neck*. The eight tapping points are: the eyebrow, side of the eye, under the eye, and under the nose, chin, collarbone, arm, and top of the head. A complete round of tapping is from the eyebrow to the top of the head. The descriptions and illustrations of the tapping points are on the next few pages.

Step 5:
Breathe, that is, inhale through your nose and exhale out of your mouth after each complete round of tapping or after successive rounds. I suggest you breathe one to three times to move that energy out. Also drink plenty of water.

Step 6:
Remeasure the level of discomfort. Tap as many rounds as needed to get your level of discomfort to 0 or at a level that satisfies you. You can tap rounds without a pause in between each round and breathe at the end.

Now that you know how to tap, are you ready to work on your relationships?

Tapping Points

Karate chop: At the center or halfway between the end of your pinky finger and your wrist on the outside of either hand. The part of your hand you would use to deliver a karate chop. Tap the karate chop point with the tip of the index finger and the middle finger or all four tips of your opposite hand.

Eyebrow: At the beginning of either eyebrow close to either side of the nose. Tap left, right or both eyebrow points.

Side of eye: Run your index finger from the beginning of eyebrow down to the end of the eyebrow to the side of eye where it meets the soft dent called the temple. Tap left, right, or both sides of the eye.

Under the eye: On the bone under the eye (either) just below the pupil.

Under the nose: The small area between the bottom of nose and above the top lip.

Chin: Halfway between the end of the bottom lip and the end of your chin.

Collarbone: The soft spot in between the collarbone. Move down one inch, and then go to the right or left one inch. Tap right or left or both sides with your index and middle fingers or make a fist and use the back side of all your fingers.

<u>Under the arm:</u> On the side of the body (either side) about four inches down from the armpit. For men, a point even with the nipple and in the middle of the bra strap for women.

<u>Top of head:</u> Put your left and right index fingers on top of each ear and run your fingers up to the top of your head. The fingers meet at the point on the top of your head.

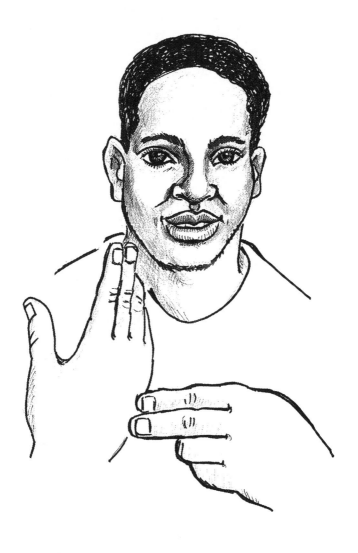

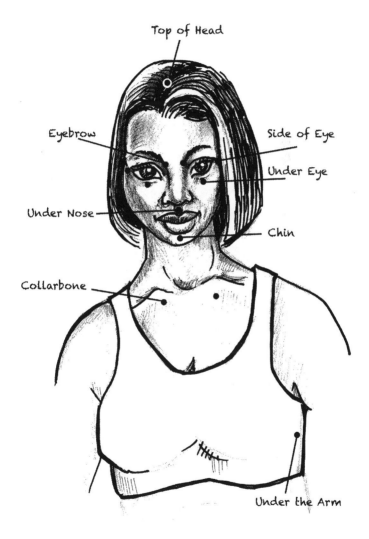

Top of Head

Eyebrow

Side of Eye

Under Eye

Under Nose

Chin

Collarbone

Under the Arm

Chapter 2

"Let's Get It On"

I once cursed love,
Vowed never to enter its turbulent doors.
Now love torments me.
My strength and heart have betrayed me.
I am a prisoner to love's unruly behavior.
It lures me only to rip my flesh.
I have bled until my body ached.
Love chastises me to no end.
I fear love's unforgiving nature.
Even though love has pierced my heart,
I reach out for my soul's only salvation,
LOVE.

—*Tyffany Howard, March 1, 2000*

I know, you thought from the title that I was going to talk about sex. Look at it this way: good sex flows out of healthy relationships. Our community doesn't openly discuss sex or sexual orientation, so I am going to tiptoe around it. Allow me to play big sister when I say that sex is one aspect to having a sustaining and loving relationship with your partner. While sexual healing is great, black couples need some relationship healing. The truth is that we don't know how to make our relationships work. After slavery, our ancestors were grateful for the opportunity to get married, have a family, and live within a community. Our ancestors knew the value of staying together and making it work. The black male and the black female were all each of them had, and they knew that they had to work together to survive. What happened? One thought is that we don't know how to love because we were not taught how to love each other. Our family structures are broken. The trauma of our ancestors being torn apart and sold—the man to one plantation, the woman to another, and the children sold to yet another plantation—is still imprinted on our DNA. Each generation continues to carry that trauma in its cellular memory even though we're no longer slaves. Then there's that much-talked-about 1712 speech of Willie Lynch. Willie Lynch, a white slave owner, delivered his speech on the James River in the Colony of Virginia, teaching slave owners a method to control their black slaves. He said, "You use the female versus the male, and the male versus the female."[3] This speech instructed further on how to break the African woman so she would become strong and independent and the black male, mentally dependent and weak but physically strong. Lynch believed that the results of this male–female role reversal, or psychological reversing process, would continue forever "unless a phenomenon occurs and reshifts the position of the male and female savages."[4] I submit to you that this phenomenon exists today and is a significant cause of the failure of black relationships.

So the black male and female were conditioned to be in opposition to each other, with the female strong and independent and the male weak and dependent. I have lived this phenomenon. Have you? My mama reared my sisters and me to be strong and independent and not to put up with anything from a black man. At the first moment of discord, he is gone. We learned that we didn't need a man to take care of us. Willie Lynch's process continues today. This notion has been depicted time and time again in black movies and music, so you know that I am not making this up. Somehow, too, the government replaced the black man. When the black man isn't around, black women qualify for government subsidies like welfare and food stamps. On a deep level, the government has conditioned black women to be without a black man in return for food and shelter. Yeah, that just came out of nowhere, but it has you scratching your head. I don't want to burst your bubble, sisters, but we all need somebody. Although the picture looks bleak, there are some black couples who stay together and raise a family. However, this chapter is about facing the problem, tracing the root cause of the problem, and replacing it with something sustainable and healthy.

Let's continue to trace the reasons for our relationship woes. From my experience, another reason for our relationship failure is that we have not been taught the skills to make our relationships work. Our education system doesn't teach us how to be happy, how to love, how to sustain a relationship, and how to resolve disagreements with loving and gentle communication.

As slaves, the black male and female were taught and allowed to breed. In my current relationship with my partner, K.Y., I am learning that communicating honestly about how I feel is empowering, freeing, healthy, and keeps the love flowing. At the age of forty-five, I am just now learning relationship skills. The first time K.Y. suggested we process our disagreement together by sharing our honest thoughts and feelings, I felt like a fish out of water. I was ready to break up because that's all I knew. On the other hand, K.Y. was conditioned to talk about her feelings in the open and not secretly resent the other person. That is revolutionary.

Our ancestors didn't have the option to love like we have today. Slaves were not allowed or taught to cultivate strong, loving relationships. If you think about it, as a slave, it would have been dangerous to fall in love. It could have meant death, beatings, or separation. Think about the stress attached to love. Then imagine having a baby that would probably be sold, beaten, or killed. Our parents could only teach us what they knew. My mama worked three or more jobs when I was growing up, so she didn't have time to sit down and teach me about love and how to make a relationship work. Since humans learn from their environment, black relationships are a product of some tough emotional wounds around love. As a result of our ancestors' trauma, which is imprinted on our DNA, it is highly probable that the black man and woman have resentment, anger, fear, grief, and sadness associated with being together.

So when the Reverend Al Green sings "Let's Stay Together," he has no idea. Instead of strong, loving black relationships and families, we have baby mamas and daddies. It is so prevalent that white folks use the term in conversation as a joke, in movies, and on the radio. Here's a possible scenario: A black man and woman get together, and the brain says, "Oh no, you know this won't work, you know master is going to sell us off. You can't protect me, you won't be here, so why should I invest in you when you won't be around and can't provide for me?" Then the black relationship falls apart.

Even though we have all that trauma from our culture's past, black folks have to accept responsibility for their stuff. What stuff is that? Here I go. Don't be mad. I am going to pull the Band-Aid off so that our wounds can get some oxygen. Another possible reason for our lack of togetherness is that as this country began to progress and integration became the norm, black communities crumbled, and the black men and black women began to not need each other like they did after slavery. Integration brought about new challenges, which created an unspoken competition between the black man and the black woman. These new societal dynamics created more advantages for black women than black men. The black woman was seen as less threatening and, thus, had greater opportunities to get jobs, get an education, and be tolerated. The image creators have continuously depicted the black man and woman in opposition. Black women raise white children and take care of white folks' homes, so they are viewed as responsible and strong, as pretty much having their professional act together, and as being the desire of white men. Black men, however, have been painted as threats to society and the establishment, cheaters, and sexual monsters who are physically strong, lazy, unintelligent, broke, and desire white women. No one discusses it, but some of our relationships feel like a competition that leads to resentment, anger, and breakups.

We have allowed others to define us and our relationships. The media, movies, television, negative music, and mostly our own thoughts sabotage our relationships. The most damaging of these are our thoughts. Stop listening to other people's negative talk about you and your relationship. Most of all, stop acting on and reacting to those fearful and negative thoughts in your head. You are not the voices in your head. It is not easy to turn off the negative self-talk, but you can learn not to listen to it. That talk may sound like, "I am not enough," "He is not good enough for me," or "She just wants my money."

Now that I have suggested some reasons why black relationships are difficult to maintain, I say we tap on the emotional wounds that we bury because we haven't been taught a healthy way to process our pain or emotions.

Note: You may want to discuss these issues with a counselor or therapist. I know, I know, black people don't go to counseling or therapy. So if counseling or therapy is not an option for you, try tapping.

Let's start with some music that fosters appreciation and love for your partner. I suggest India.Arie's "Moved by You," Beyonce's "Halo," or Eric Benet and Tamia's "Spend My Life with You." Once the music has touched your soul, start tapping.

Tap on Your Relationships

Think about a current relationship or a past relationship. Once you have the relationship, play it in your mind like it is a movie. Then measure the level of discomfort from 0 to 10. When my ex-husband and I ended our twelve-year relationship, I felt hurt, anger, fear, sadness, and resentment. When I thought about our relationship, my level of intensity was an eight. After tapping on the hurt and fear, my level dropped to a three. Remember, the results are different for each person.

Describe your relationship problem in the form of a setup statement like you learned in chapter 1. If you are too rattled and can't really describe the problem, here are some sample problems to get you started tapping:

- Even though I have this resentment that (your partner's name) can't provide for me, I deeply and completely love and accept myself.
- Even though this relationship scares me, I deeply and completely love and accept myself.
- Even though I have this trust issue, I deeply and completely love and accept myself.

To practice, let's tap three times on the karate chop point: "Even though this relationship scares me, I deeply and completely love and accept myself." Then, while tapping on the eight points, we will repeat the short phrase, "This relationship scares me."

eyebrow—this relationship scares me
side of eye—this relationship scares me
under the eye—this relationship scares
under the nose—this relationship scares me
chin—this relationship scares me

collarbone—this relationship scares me
under the arm—this relationship scares me
top of head—this relationship scares me

Complete as many tapping rounds as you like. After each round, breathe. Don't forget to remeasure your level of discomfort after each round. Yay! You have officially tapped that! It wasn't so bad, was it? How do you feel? Now that you have done a little work on your relationships, how about we stop trippin'?

Chapter 3

Why You Trippin'?

Special Note to Readers: I didn't write this chapter to cause harm, insult, offend, or attack anyone. My intent is to bring light to an issue that America doesn't talk about, deal with, or tell the truth about. This is about some of the experiences that African Americans endure on a daily basis. African Americans receive no therapy, no counseling, and no medium to address how they feel. It's about African Americans healing. Blacks and whites have to accept responsibility for the role that they play. If you feel guilty about something, deal with it in a healthy way. All black folks don't feel this way, and all white folks are not racists. I advocate love and forgiveness, which involve honest dialogue.

Stress kills, especially in our community. Along with the typical stressors of having or not having a job, family responsibilities, health issues, securing shelter, having enough food to eat, and being gunned down by overzealous cops, African Americans have to deal with the stress that no one wants to address: racism. Let's be honest, some white people stress us out! Even the open-minded white folks stress us out because we don't know what their angle is and when they are going to start trippin'. I read a lot of spiritually centered books, and none of them dares to discuss our racial divide or offer solutions to heal the wounds. No one talks about it, but we have a love-hate relationship with white folks. Our relationship with white folks is like a child's relationship with his parents. We seek white folks' approval, we want to make them happy, and we want them to notice when we do something good or that we are not like "the other black folks." When we are treated badly by some white people, we do nothing because there could be severe consequences. In Texas, a black person could find himself or herself shot dead or dragged behind a truck. The way we are treated causes so much stress for us.

For example, I had a best girlfriend who would come and visit my ex-husband and me on the weekends when we lived in Belton, Texas. She would spend the weekend talking about the crazy white folks at her job. We discussed how they, white folks, will try to sabotage you; they have different expectations for you from other people because you are African American. Some white people, thinking themselves clever, will couch their true feelings about African Americans in a joke and tell it to the only African American at the office, assuming that he or she is too dumb to get it. Black comedians often joke that African Americans must be overly educated with two or three degrees to the white person's no degree or one degree. At the workplace, you have to tiptoe around them because they will fire you, demote you, or embarrass you at the drop of a hat. We always have to watch our backs because white people will make up stuff to get you in trouble. Again, black comedians joke about these everyday situations because they know, by and large, that these are the experiences of blacks across America. And the blacks in the audience will confirm the familiarity of the joke by laughing, nodding their heads yes, and clapping. Together, my friend, ex-husband, and I have seven degrees, and we were still consumed with the stress and unease brought on by white people.

For many blacks, the weekends are both a time to sigh because they are out of the particular stressful environment and a time to gear up for the following week. You know how you feel Sunday night. In our homes, churches, and get-togethers, almost every conversation will include a discussion about how we are treated by white people. How they treat us on the job, at the grocery store, in the mall, at the bank, anywhere and everywhere. Think how much we worry about what we will have to change about ourselves to make them feel comfortable. Will they be fair? Will we have to pretend to be interested in the stuff that they talk about? How much will we have to kiss their butt? How long before they attack? Will our grammar be perfect enough? Will they approve of us? And on and on. Our experiences and interactions with white people have traumatized us so much that we have become obsessed to the point of being mentally and physically ill. I don't know about you, but I am exhausted. Many blacks have an amazing skill in that we can assess the moods of white people. You know what I mean. We know when it's time to get out of their presence. Our ancestors were in tune to the slave owners' emotions and mood swings because they had to be in order to survive.

Allow me to illustrate my point. I make my living primarily as a criminal defense attorney. This work is highly stressful and produces so much anxiety. As an African American female lawyer, I have to deal with a lot of challenges. The justice system is slow, outdated, and broken. In Texas, African Americans are about 11 percent of the population but make up almost of 40 percent of the prison population. I live in a rural area of central Texas. There are about six African American attorneys practicing criminal defense. My ex-husband is also a criminal defense attorney. He is an intelligent, competent, and talented trial attorney who is treated like he is subhuman. It is painful to watch. However, you can't allow someone's ignorance to weigh you down and define who you are. When I go to the courthouse and am in front of a judge with an African American court officer or bailiff, I ask, "So how's your judge today?" Because I know that the court officer has watched the judge's demeanor, feels his or her energy, and has studied on a daily basis the judge's moods. When the court officer responds to my question with "keep it short," I know the judge is in a pissy mood and will act up. If it is one of those days, I know I have to come across meek and nonthreatening. All that kowtowing makes me sick.

I may have stepped on some toes, and to be honest, I don't care. Our country refuses to have an honest dialogue about racism so I thought I would get one started. Ignoring this tough problem doesn't mean it will go away. And creating an environment in which individuals talk about the negative effects of racism is oppressive. I don't have any published studies about the effects of racism on blacks' well-being. I don't need a study. My family and friends live it, and so do I. My ex-husband would often say about racism, "Those who feel it, know it." I am no different from any other African American in America to the extent that I have to deal with the challenges of my job and the stress created because someone has a hang-up with my gender, skin color, and now that I came out in this book, my sexual orientation. What are some healthy ways to deal with the physical and mental manifestations of stress as it relates to racism, your job, and just living the human condition? You must learn to love and forgive yourself and others. Love all living beings and understand that when people treat you in unloving ways, it has nothing to do with you; it goes to their level of consciousness. It is difficult, but don't take it personally and hold space for them with love and light. Remember that good people come in all colors, shapes, and sizes, so let go of judgment. Realize that you are not a victim. Regain your power by voicing your truth in loving, productive, and creative ways.

This chapter has covered some heavy stuff, so I am about ready to tap. Before we begin tapping, I wanted to share a story about my sister Reshena. She's forty-two and works in the records department for a cardiologist clinic. The stress from her working environment would cause her to have headaches every day at work. One weekend, I stayed with her at her apartment. On Sunday night, before I left to go back home, I taught her to tap to relieve her headaches. Around six o'clock Monday evening, Reshena called me, excited. She told me enthusiastically, "Tyffany, guess what? I tapped this morning before going to work, and I didn't get a headache all day." Then she thanked me for teaching her how to tap. I was so happy that I was able to share something I learned with my sister and that she used it to relieve her physical pain.

Tap on Stress and Anxiety

Did that story about my sister or anything discussed in this chapter resonate with you? You know your experiences better than I do, so tap on those. Otherwise, here are some sample problems that you may want to tap on:

- Even though I have this stress from the man always on my back, I deeply and completely love and accept myself.
- Even though I have this anxiety from always being looked at as less than, I deeply and completely love and accept myself.
- Even though I have this headache, I deeply and completely love and accept myself.

Measure your level of discomfort. Next, karate chop three times: "Even though I have this stress from the man always on my back, I deeply and completely love and accept myself." Tap on the meridian endpoints, repeating the short phrase provided for you as a sample below. After you have completed a round, breathe. You can always tap more than one round and use one or both hands to tap. If you tap continuous rounds, you can breathe at the end.

eyebrow—this stress
side of eye—this stress
under the eye—this stress
under the nose—this stress
chin—this stress
collarbone—this stress
under the arm—this stress
top of head—this stress

That is enough of stress and anxiety. Don't forget to drink some water. Are you ready to discover how you are all that and a bag of chips?

Chapter 4

You're All That and a Bag of Chips

I remember when "Video" by India.Arie came out. I said to myself, "Wow, what an empowering song." That song helped me learn to appreciate and accept myself as God made me. Whenever someone asks me why I wear my hair just like it comes out of my head, naturally curly, I think of that song. The lyrics resonated with me. India sings, "I know my creator didn't make no mistakes on me." She is right about that, but most of you don't believe it. Even the response you give people when they ask how you are, and you say, "Blessed and highly favored," seems to be a mechanical response. That is, most of you just repeat it like a parrot, but you don't believe it or live it. Then you say you believe in God, but some of you question God's choice of nose, lips, hair, and skin color. I am just going to go ahead and say it: black people hate themselves. Yes, I am going there. As a matter of fact, some of you hate yourself so much that you can't stand to look at other black people because they remind you of you. They remind you of everything the image creators have taught you to dislike about yourself.

From what I have observed, African Americans have a cultural core belief. That core belief is "we are not enough." This belief plays itself out in the way we treat each other and ourselves. When communicating, we may sometimes tell another African American, "You ain't sh★★." Or when an African American is looking at us, we will ask that person, "What are you looking at?" Sometimes that question leads to an altercation. One of the most common ways the core belief that "we are not enough" plays out is when we see a black person and that person doesn't speak. African Americans, young or old, rich or poor, educated or uneducated, light skinned or dark skinned, know that not speaking is like spitting in someone's face. What are the possible reasons for not speaking? They think that they are better than you, or they don't want white people to think that they know you, or they want to be the only black person getting the attention or being noticed by white people, or they don't want to be reminded that they are black. The belief that you are not enough, and culturally we are not enough, affects so many aspects of our lives—relationships, income, unhealthy lifestyles, treatment of others, and lack of love for self. Self-love and self-acceptance are key to generating dramatic shifts in our everyday lives. Our community is literally starving in the love department. We weren't taught how to love each other and ourselves. Self-love is not as easy as just saying, "I love myself." But that does help and is a great start. Every morning before I get in the shower, I look in the bathroom mirror and say three times, "Tyffany, I love you, I really love you." From my experience, self-love requires positive self-talk and a daily commitment to learning who you are and accepting that person with gentleness. The reason I am stressing the point about self-love is because the lack of love for self is tied to so much suffering in the world. For example, when you love yourself, you choose to be in healthy relationships, you have no desire to harm others, you see love in others, you care about what you put in your body and mind, and you see more possibilities. When you are in love with yourself, you know that you are not how much money you have, where you live, your skin color, your nose, your lips, or your hair.

That leads me to a discussion about our feelings about our hair. So let's talk about black hair. If I made the statement that black people are preoccupied and maybe even obsessed with their hair, would that be an exaggeration? I don't think so. Chris Rock's movie *Good Hair* was very telling. The preoccupation with the texture of the hair that comes out of your head is some more of that self-hate and "I am not enough" crap. If I hear one more black person comment on good hair vs. bad hair, I am going to scream. Black people, especially black women, will go to any length to fry, dye, or lay to the side the hair that comes out of their heads. We criticize each other's hair choices. It is just hair, people. Truth is, you hate your hair because somebody told you that black hair is not pleasing to white people, that it is *bad* if it is not whacked off or straight. We little black girls and boys hear the negative talk and see the images that encourage altering our physical features; those are messages that teach our kids that they are not enough. Again, that core belief has not served us well. India.Arie nailed it with her song "I Am Not My Hair." No other ethnic group is as consumed with their hair, lips, nose, and skin color as we are. We broadcast to the world how we feel about being black in our attitudes, behavior, and treatment of ourselves and other black people. We show the world that we believe that we are not enough. Think about your earliest memory of when you felt that you were not enough. Mainstream America tells us every day that we are not enough—that our hair, nose, lips, and skin color are not enough. That is oppression. Blacks have experienced so much oppression that we oppress each other and ourselves. Aren't you tired of hating what you look like? Are you ready to accept yourself and accept that you are more than the hair that comes out of your head or the skin that covers your earth suit? Even though black people are no longer in physical bondage, we continue to enslave ourselves with all the negative beliefs about who we are. You have forgotten your greatness, so allow me to remind you of how great you are.

Some years ago when I ran for judge, the Temple, Texas, chapter of the NAACP asked me to be the guest speaker for its annual senior scholarship dinner. I gave a speech based on Og Mandino's book *The Greatest Miracle in the World*. If you have not read this book, you are missing out. What a glorious piece of work! Og Mandino writes:

> "You have no memory of that moment when
> first you emerged from your mother's womb
> and I placed my hand on your soft brow. And

the secret I whispered in your small ear when I bestowed my blessings upon you! "Let me share with you, again, the secret you heard at your birth and forgot. You are my greatest miracle. You are the greatest miracle in the world. Those were the first words you ever heard. Then you cried."[5]

Black people, you along with all human beings, are God's greatest miracle. God didn't exclude you from the fold. You and the unloved, that is, those other people who are in so much pain because they don't believe that they are enough so they take it out on you, excluded you from the miracle of being great. Your beautiful array of skin color, your full lips, your curly hair, and your strong round nose were chosen for you. There is only one beautiful you so be proud. Not only are you God's greatest miracle but you are also a little god. The ego, or the mind-made self, has convinced you that you are separate from God. Ego means to ease God out. You are not separate from God or any other living being. In Exodus 3:14, Moses asked God (the burning bush) what his name was, and God said, "I am that I am …"[6] That means, *I am that* animal, tree, earth, sky, ocean, neighbor, boss, person, experience. You!

So when you destroy yourself with self-hate, you go against God. I know that it is difficult for you to believe that you are beautiful when all the propaganda says otherwise. The sooner you realize that the media does not have your best interest at heart, the better off you will be. Don't fall for the "programming." Someone defined beauty and plastered it everywhere and decided that it wasn't you.

Then you fell for the image brainwash. Maybe no one has ever told you that you are beautiful. You don't have to wait for someone to tell you. Make it an affirmation, and tell yourself every day that you are beautiful. I do. My suggestion is to stop being a slave to others' definition of you and to what they think about you. Everything that the Divine Spirit created is beautiful. Can I get an amen? I will give it to myself. Amen, Tyffany. I can't make you believe that you are all that and a bag of chips. You are beautiful! Yes, even Miss Sealy. Once you go within and stop looking for validation outside of yourself, you will see the beauty that is you. Do you feel me?

Tap in Self-Love and Acceptance

Anybody feel like tapping on some of the problems I have addressed in this chapter? Maybe your physical features and self-love are not problems for you. Then be honest with yourself about whatever is preventing you from accepting yourself and tap on that. Measure your level of discomfort. If you can't think of anything, try these problem statements.

- Even though I have this tightly curled hair, I deeply and completely love and accept myself anyway.
- Even though I have this belief that I'm not enough, I deeply and completely love and accept myself anyway.
- Even though I have this brown skin that I accept and don't accept, I completely love and accept myself anyway.

Tap on the karate chop three times, "Even though I have this belief that I'm not enough, I deeply and completely love and accept myself anyway." Then tap on the meridian endpoints, reciting the short phrase.

eyebrow—this belief that I'm not enough
side of eye—this belief that I'm not enough
under the eye—this belief that I'm not enough
under the nose—this belief that I'm not enough
chin—this belief that I'm not enough
collarbone—this belief that I'm not enough
under the arm—this belief that I'm not enough
top of head—this belief that I'm not enough

After you have tapped a complete round, remeasure your level of discomfort. If you are not at a 0, tap another round. Let's say you are at a 3; tap on the remaining 3 like so: "Even though I have this remaining 3, I deeply and completely love and accept myself." Tap on the meridian end points and breathe. Next, how about we tap on some of that anger and fear?

Chapter 5

"You Told Harpo to Beat Me?"

Anger and fear are not our enemies. Both emotions can be useful in alerting us to danger. However, anger and fear become problems when you allow them to control you rather than controlling them. When do you get angry or afraid? Is it around a certain person or when you are treated a certain way? I get angry when I am treated unfairly, disrespected, or feel powerless. I will hold on to my anger for days, months, and sometimes years. Usually, I am most angry with myself for not speaking my truth. From my experience, when you hold on to fear and anger, that is a clear sign that fear and anger are controlling you. The reason I have lumped fear and anger together is because fear is at the root of anger.

Many of you have probably been told that fear is not real. That is true, but our mind makes it real. The best illustration of the point I am attempting to make is the movie *The Matrix*. For those of you who have seen it, you will remember the scene when Neo is about to make the jump that no one else has made. Morpheus tells Neo that it is all in his mind, that Neo has to believe he can do it. That it is a computer program and not real. Well, what happens? Neo jumps and lands on his face, and his mouth is filled with blood. Neo looks at Morpheus and says something like "I thought you said that it wasn't real." Morpheus responds, "Your mind makes it real." Our brain created fear as an evolutionary-instinctual response to alert humans living in the caveman era to run when they saw something that could kill them. Throughout evolution, fear has warned us of possible dangers to our physical survival. And fear arises when there is any kind of perceived threat, even though there may not be any physical danger. For instance, fear arises when we don't have enough money to pay a bill, when we might be evicted, or when we ask someone to marry us. That is because the brain cannot distinguish between a real physical threat and an unreal threat to survival. Also, fear rears its head when there is a threat to your ego, which we call your personal identity. When there is a perceived threat to your personal identity, fear arises and the brain works to find a way to protect you. Each one of us has a personal identity whose job is to boss us around. A personal identity is your mind-made self. It is a false perception of who you really are. Your ego or mind tells you that you are this or that, and you believe it, defend it, and walk around as if that's who you really are. This will be an aha moment, so please wait for it. Whenever it is a verbal argument, an embarrassing situation, a public-speaking activity, or any situation where you are not being physically threatened and fear shows its face, that is a signal to defend and protect your personal identity, your ego. Your personal identity is the made-up story about you and your life. Then society and your family confirm that's who you are, and you believe it. I want you to really get this point so I feel that I need to break it down some more. A superhero wears a cape, a colorful suit, and a mask and has an attitude that goes along with the costume. Underneath the mask and costume is the true self. Even though we don't wear costumes, our mind/ego creates a mask, an attitude, and a costume for us—our personal identity. When the ego feels threatened by someone finding out that our costume is not real, it becomes scared. Sometimes that fear manifests into anger, arrogance, pride, or worry. Those emotions are shields we use to protect ourselves because we are afraid. Don't look at fear as being something bad. Fear, like anger, can be beneficial to you if channeled in the right way. Look at these emotions as a compass pointing you in the direction that you should go. When fear or anger arise, view the situation as an opportunity to learn and grow, an opportunity to heal something within yourself. Also, take the time to ask yourself, "Is there a physical danger, and if not, what am I afraid of?" You are not being chased by lions so the perceived danger is emotional, which means you have options to deal with it. I have a great courtroom story to illustrate my point about anger and fear.

I had a jury trial in 2010. My client was charged with a state jail felony, which is punishable by serving 180 days to two years in state jail. But my client had prior felony convictions that enhanced the punishment to that of a second-degree felony, which meant that he was looking at two to twenty years in prison. As a criminal defense lawyer, my job is to represent my client, and in doing that job, I have to fight the prosecutor and, most times, the judge as well. Why would I have to fight the judge? Subconsciously, the judge is partial to the state. Anyway, this case was one of those times. I made an objection about some evidence that couldn't come in, and the judge called the lawyers to the bench. At the bench, the judge with such pride responded to my pleas of justice with words I will never forget. He said that he didn't believe in justice. But it wasn't that statement that ticked me off. What ticked my ego off is that the judge didn't make one ruling in my favor. At one point, he dismissed the jury to chastise me about how I was trying the case. When I gave him that black woman's "you don't know who you are talking to" look, the judge, who stood at least six feet tall to my five feet three inches, yelled, "Don't you look at me like I am the big bad judge trying to intimidate you." Boy, was I pissed! I was angry because he was intimidating me and wasn't being fair and impartial, and the only response I could give without getting myself into trouble was "Yes, Your Honor." The judge's court officer, or bailiff, and people sitting in the gallery whom I didn't know told me at a recess that the judge was helping the state and treating me badly. My ego told me, "You are being attacked, so defend yourself." I didn't know what to do other than be angry and feel wounded. That judge's disrespect for what I thought I was—a polished, confident trial attorney, someone to be respected—deflated my balloon. To tell the truth, I was angrier with me because I didn't stick up for myself. I didn't have the courage to tell the judge that he was an arrogant, unfair, no-count judge. I began to question my abilities as a trial attorney, got depressed, and turned on myself by mentally telling myself that I was a coward. Then I realized that fear was lurking beneath the anger. I was afraid of the judge, what he could do to my career, what he could do to my client, and what he would think of me because my ego believed I was thought of as a competent black lawyer who didn't cause problems. Truth is, I feared not being liked. Wow! That made me even angrier with myself, because I wanted to be seen as the lawyer who fought the establishment and called a spade a spade. But also, I had uncovered a deep dark secret that only my ego knew about: I wanted the judge to like me. In fact, when the judge tore into me, it triggered a childhood wound of being unloved and not enough, which caused me to become angry and afraid. The anger and fear ate at me for three years. As I am writing about this experience, I realize that by sharing it with you, I am now forgiving that judge and, more importantly, forgiving myself. I must love him because to love him is to love myself. Also, I realize that I turned on myself instead of finding an outlet for my anger and fear. I didn't know then how to release it. No, I could not curse the judge out or beat him like Harpo beat Miss Sophia in *The Color Purple*. I wanted to, and he knew it. Although I lost so much respect for that judge, when he retired, I gave him the book *Only Love is Real* by Dr. Brian Weiss. On the inside cover, I thanked him for teaching me how to be courageous and stand up to anyone, especially a judge. By that time I had realized that the judge, like me, had fallen victim to his ego and was only doing the best that he could at his level of consciousness.

Looking back, if I knew about tapping, I would have been able to use it to release the anger and fear, and maybe I would not have gotten depressed and tortured myself. We can't continue to turn anger and fear inward on ourselves because it is harmful and doesn't serve us. Now, I want you to think of any experience involving anger or fear. You may still be angry. Together, we are going to tap on it. Here are some sample anger and fear problem statements.

- Even though I have this anger toward (<u>the person's name</u>), I deeply and completely love and accept myself.
- Even though I have this fear of speaking up for myself, I deeply and completely love and accept myself.
- Even though I have this anger about (the problem), I deeply and completely love and accept myself.

As always, you may use the problem statement provided or tap on the problems that are present in your life. I strongly recommend that you visualize the problems from your own experiences and tap on them.

Tapping Down Fear and Anger

Start with the problem statement, "Even though I have this anger about this problem, I deeply and completely love and accept myself." Did you remember to measure your level of discomfort? Now, tap on the karate chop point three times while reciting the problem statement.

Next, tap on the meridian endpoints as you recite the short phrase "this anger."

> eyebrow—this anger
> side of eye—this anger
> under the eye—this anger
> under the nose—this anger
> chin—this anger
> under the arm—this anger
> collarbone—this anger
> top of head—this anger

Have you reduced your anger and fear? If one round is enough for you, breathe, drink some water, and remeasure your level of discomfort. No, one round wasn't enough? Then tap more than one round without a break between the rounds and wait to breathe at the end. I need you to be calm for the next chapter. We have to go deep, and by deep I mean our past. Are you ready to tackle how you feel about slavery? Have a little faith!

Chapter 6

We Have Come This Far by Faith

Destiny is not a matter of chance but a
matter of choice. It lies right
here in our hands.
And we can become what we want to be …

—*William Jennings Bryant*

Slavery happened! However, like anger and fear, if you allow your feelings about it to control every aspect of your life, you will not move forward. Are you attached to our past as a group whose ancestors were enslaved? If you are, ask yourself what the benefit is to hanging on to those negative emotions and what you lose by letting those feelings go. Do you believe that by hanging on to those feelings you honor our ancestors, and if you let them go, they would be dishonored? Is it because you prefer to be known as a victim, or is it because you think that the world will forget? Is it because you want to use slavery as a crutch and an excuse for you not moving forward in life? Whatever your reason for hanging on to the past, know that slavery is a stain that can never simply be washed away just by you releasing its hold on you. Although an absolute human rights nightmare, slavery made us stronger. We are resilient. The fact that we, a people whose ancestors were enslaved, survived the challenges that followed from slavery is something that we should be proud of. That being said, slavery is a treacherous story of the past and not who we are. Your true self, your soul, is who you are, and your soul is not and will never be a slave. Black folks are not the only ones who still live in the past. Some white folks still relish the good old days when we picked cotton and walked around saying, "Yes, sir, massa Tom."

You may not feel like laughing, but to illustrate my point, I want to share a hilarious story about people who just can't let the ignorance go. I still laugh about the time my mom's boss lost his mind. One of my mom's bosses, a wealthy white man, invited my ex-husband and me over to his house to discuss some business. He was starting a singles' dating website and thought we could help him get the African American singles market. Anyway, we sat on his porch in the beautiful suburb of Westlake in Austin, Texas, chatting about business and our backgrounds. We black folks call it "white boy poker." If you are not privy to this terminology, white boy poker is when some white folks ask you questions about what you do to size you up so they can put you in a box or compare their success to yours. Well, it was a nice sunny afternoon. We were all playing nice, talking about law school and how my law practice was going. This guy and I graduated from the same law school, the University of Houston Law Center in Houston, Texas, and my ex-husband graduated from the Thurgood Marshall School of Law, which is also in Houston. Out of nowhere, this man opens his mouth and asks me whether I had picked cotton to pay for law school. My ex-husband and I looked at each other like this guy had lost his mind. I replied, "No!" After that question, I knew it was time to go. We chatted for a few more minutes and then told this guy that we had somewhere else to be. On our way home, my ex-husband and I laughed and talked about that sad, pitiful man. We started singing, "Oh Lordy, pick a bale of cotton. Oh Lordy, pick a bale a day," whenever we thought of that experience and needed a laugh. This story is just a reminder that wealth and education are not substitutes for kindness, compassion, or character.

Why did I tell you that story about my mom's boss? Because we need to tell the truth about what we experience, and sometimes you have to nudge people to do the right thing by exposing their mean-spirited behavior to the world. For me, healing requires sharing experiences that may make people uncomfortable. Healing is not pretty or easy, nor does it come in a perfect little package. It takes courage to forgive the people who enslaved our ancestors, profited from their enslavement, destroyed black families, and raped, murdered, and disassembled a rich culture. But we must forgive and love all those involved in the slave trade and ownership of slaves, and that includes Africans, too. Also, you cannot lump all white folks together in a bucket. All white people aren't the same, and they aren't all out to keep you down and harm you. And you may not want to hear this, but we, all living things, are all connected. Even though humans attempt to separate themselves from each other, from other living beings and from God, there is no separation. As India.Arie sings, "We Are One." So whatever your reason for living in the past, it is holding you back. How does the past keep you from moving forward? When you live in the past, you are resistant to the present. And when you are resistant to the present, it is difficult to flow with change and difficult to be aware of opportunities that are right in your face. Too much living in the past creates confusion, depression, fear, anger, sadness, and grief. The brain can't make a distinction between the past and the present, so even though you know that an event happened hundreds of years ago, the brain doesn't. Those emotions cause the body to be in a state of constant stress and trauma. Stress and trauma means our bodies are not in harmony and balance. When our bodies are not in harmony and balance, we become ill.

Knowing where we came from isn't a bad thing. In fact, the past is useful for measuring how far we have come and for reminding us that humans can behave horribly and we must stay alert. However, when the past becomes debilitating, it is time to put the past into perspective. Accept that the US government may never apologize— and I don't see any reparations being disbursed anytime soon. Slavery was deplorable, ungodly, and a stain on our country. No one is saying that slavery was okay or that you are weak for wanting to live in the present moment. With all that African Americans have endured, know that you can't heal, live out your life's purpose, or be abundant and truly free when you live in the past. The past no longer serves you. By living in the present moment, you are saying yes to life and yes to where you are right now.

African Americans are much greater than being the descendants of slaves. Like all life, we are divine. So stop blaming white people for everything! It is not healthy, it is not loving yourself, it is not loving God, and it keeps you in the powerless state of being a victim. There are people in this world who do bad things, and knowing that, you still choose to live to your full potential. Because if you don't live to your fullest potential, that is a sin. Decide now to create the life that you want to live.

This issue may be too big for tapping. If you find that the emotions that you are experiencing are too complex for tapping, please consult the appropriate health-care professional. This book is only an introductory guide to tapping and is not meant to resolve complex traumas. For those of you who would like to tap, here are some sample problem statements that may resonate with you.

- Even though I have this grief, I deeply and completely love and accept myself.
- Even though I have this anger toward them for what they did, I completely love and accept myself.
- Even though I don't see a benefit to holding on to my feelings, I want to hold onto them, and I am okay with that.

Tap through the Past

Begin with the karate chop point and tap three times reciting the problem statement, "Even though I have this anger toward them for what they did, I completely love and accept myself." Then tap on the endpoints.

> eyebrow—this anger
> side of eye—toward them
> under the eye—for what they did
> under the nose—this anger
> chin—toward them
> collarbone—for what they did
> under the arm—this anger
> top of head—for what they did

After completing a round or rounds, remeasure your level of discomfort. *If and only if your level of discomfort is a three or less,* try tapping this problem statement, "Even though I don't want to forgive them, I'm willing to forgive them so I can move forward." The sequence is provided for you. The reason you shouldn't tap on this forgiveness statement if you are not ready to forgive is because it wouldn't be productive for you. It's okay if you aren't ready to forgive.

> eyebrow—I don't want to forgive
> side of eye—I'm willing to forgive
> under the eye—to move forward
> under the nose—I don't want to forgive
> chin—I'm willing to forgive
> collarbone—to move forward
> under the arm—I don't want to forgive
> top of head—I'm willing to forgive

Once you have gotten this far, take a break. Breathe and drink some water. You may even want to sit still or pray. I'm really proud of you for walking with me on this journey. It's not over. Are you ready for some of that sweet potato pie?

Chapter 7

Give Me Some of That Sweet Potato Pie

Boy, do I love sweet potato pie and key lime too! What about you? Allow me to ask you some additional questions. What do you crave? What time of day do you eat all that unhealthy food? What are you feeling emotionally when you reach for that cake, ice cream, or Snickers? Food is necessary; however, it becomes a problem for us when we abuse it and use it to comfort us. Do you use food to self-medicate like I do? For instance, sometimes I eat unhealthy foods to cope with stress or anxiety. Other times, I reach for those vegan oatmeal cookies because I am feeling unloved and those cookies comfort me. To soothe my feelings of loneliness, I grab the organic extra dark chocolate. The truth is sometimes I eat unhealthy foods because something happens that brings up feelings that I am not good enough. It could be something someone said or a mistake I made, or it could be I'm thinking that I am not where I should be in terms of my career or a relationship. Whenever I eat unhealthy, I have a little talk with myself. I say, "Tyffany, you know this stuff isn't good for you. Don't be a slave to your emotions." Then I gently and lovingly tell myself, "You are eating this stuff because you are feeling stressed, worried, and unloved." Once I have that tough love talk with myself, I go running or I juice some organic strawberries, oranges, and red grapes. Delicious! Not only is the juice healthy, it satisfies my sweet tooth and my emotional needs, and I don't feel guilty.

Can you pinpoint the first experience you had overeating? It may have started when you were a child and told to eat everything on your plate. You may have heard your mama say in a stern voice, "Boy, you'd better eat everything on your plate. We don't waste food around here. I worked hard so you could eat." You learned to eat to get full rather than eat until your stomach was satisfied. Those experiences created triggers for you that may become activated when you sit down to eat, see food, smell food, or do any activity where there is food. You are the only one who knows what your triggers are.

As you already know, obesity, high blood pressure, heart disease, and diabetes are not kind to black folks. Knowing that we have these health challenges is a warning to us to watch what we eat. Most of us have not been educated about what is best for our health. In our community, eating greasy fried foods is part of our daily staple. I'm going to throw out some ideas about our food choices. For instance, maybe you eat chitterlings, pigs' feet, and hog maws because we are attached to a belief that these foods make us black, that is, that the food is associated with our culture. Think about what our ancestors may have eaten when they were enslaved. The slave owner provided the food, which quite possibly happened to be anything left over from the pig or cow or anything not particularly delectable and nutritious. My point is that these foods have nothing to do with African American culture. They are foods eaten as a result of our environment conditioning. I'm telling you that you can change what you eat and don't have to hold on to some false belief that you're not black unless you eat chitterlings. Let's make good health, nutritious foods, and exercise part of our culture.

Yes, I said exercise. Why don't more African Americans exercise? One reason could be that the average African American is trying to find a job or maybe has one to two jobs, which makes it difficult to exercise. For many sisters juggling a job and the kids without a partner, exercise is the last thing on their minds. Another reason is physical laziness. And there are those who just don't want to exercise. I have heard all the excuses. It really sounds like more of that "I don't love myself" rap that goes on in our heads. When I was growing up, my mama had several jobs, took care of three kids, and always found time to walk three to four times a week. At sixty-four years of age, my mama still walks. Seeing my mama exercise encouraged me to exercise. African Americans are great at taking care of their spiritual needs, but when it comes to our health, we get a grade of F. When you eat healthy, exercise, and take time to be still and silent, you tell your soul that you love yourself. I will keep saying it: African Americans must learn to love themselves. It is a great feeling to be in love with yourself. I will let you in on a little secret. We have the ability to change our eating and lifestyle habits, but it will take a little work. That being said, are you excited about tapping on your food and exercise problems? As always, you may create your own problem statements or use the statements provided. See what you think about these samples:

- Even though I should exercise and I don't want to, I deeply and completely love and accept myself anyway.
- Even though I have this feeling of loneliness and I eat chocolate, I deeply and completely love and accept myself anyway.
- Even though I have this craving when I don't feel good about myself, I completely accept myself anyway.

Tap for Health

Before we start tapping for health, let's take a moment to listen to Whitney Houston's "The Greatest Love of All." Whitney sings, "Learning to love yourself is the greatest love of all." Now that you have rocked Whitney, think about your issues with food and exercise. Measure your level of intensity. Then tap on your own problem statement or use this one: "Even though I have this craving when I don't feel good about myself, I completely accept myself anyway." After three times on the karate chop point, move on to the endpoints tapping on the phrase "this craving."

eyebrow—this craving
side of eye—I don't feel good
under the eye—this craving
under the nose—I don't feel good
chin—this craving
collarbone—I don't feel good
under the arm—this craving
top of head—I don't feel good

When you've completed a round or rounds, breathe, drink some water and remeasure your intensity level. How did that tapping session feel? Did you put those cookies in the trash? It is not that easy to stop the cravings and give up your food blanket, but if you take baby steps, you will reach the mountaintop. We have reached our last chapter. Anyone want to guess what the topic is? I will give you a hint. It's green, and you can buy stuff with it. Go ahead and turn the page; mo' money is waiting for you.

Chapter 8

Mo' Money, Mo' Money

So you want more money. Money is energy that flows and the energy can be blocked so you need to be a channel for receiving more of it. Every time I spend or receive money, I say out loud, "Money is love!" I know most of us have been told by our parents or grandparents that "money is the root of all evil." That is not true. The Bible actually says that the "love" of money is the root of all evil. You can love money in a way that makes you greedy, and you can love money in a way that makes you a hoarder. Either way, if you believe that money is the root of all evil or that because you are black, you are not meant to have more money than you will ever need, then expect to continue to live paycheck to paycheck. Those beliefs are limiting and blocking the flow of money coming to you. In fact, those statements are called "limiting beliefs." Jack Canfield and Pamela Bruner, authors of *Tapping into Ultimate Success*, define a limiting belief as any belief that doesn't serve you, weakens you, or stops you from taking action toward your success.[7] How many of you have said or thought, "I am not smart enough, I don't have enough, or I am black." Those are limiting beliefs, and the truth is that those beliefs don't reflect the true nature of the universe. You attract what you think about all the time. The universe doesn't know that poverty is bad and wealth is good. All the universe knows is that you keep thinking and thinking about not having enough money, so the universe works to give you what you are putting your energy and attention on: *not having enough money*. Let's look at my friend Catherine's attitude toward money and my old attitude toward money. Catherine, my former law partner, is married and has three children. The old Tyffany didn't know any better, so she let thoughts of not having enough money run amuck in her head. In the past, I would worry myself into a crazy frenzy of not sleeping, biting my nails, and judging myself because I feared not having enough money to provide for my needs and buy some of stuff that I wanted. I was even scared to spend money because I believed that I might not have enough in the future. The fear consumed me so much that I believed the universe produced a limited supply of money to go around for everyone. At the time, my belief is what blocked my flow of money and abundance. To recap, I had a false belief that money was scarce, which ruled my lack programming. Now, my friend Catherine viewed money totally opposite from the way I looked at money. She believes that she is abundant and that there is a constant and unlimited supply of money. Every time she receives money from any source, she says, "Thank you, universe; money is love." Catherine's belief in the unlimited flow of money is so strong that she just throws checks in her desk drawer and goes months without depositing them in the bank. Once I asked her why she waits so long to deposit her checks, and she replied, "I am so abundant that I have enough money in the bank, so I don't need to deposit my checks." It's maybe silly to some people, but she even has a money dance that she does when she receives money. A few years ago, I reevaluated my beliefs about money and concluded that my beliefs had no basis in the truth. Here's another lesson: you block your money flow when you are not grateful for what you already have and when you are not accepting of little things, like a compliment. For me, compliments don't feel comfortable and are really difficult to accept. However, I realized that if I can't accept something as small as a compliment, I'm not ready to receive something great. Most of us have been taught that it is better to give than receive; however, energy has to flow in both directions. For balance, the flow of energy is to give and to receive. When you are in the mode of receiving, accept by saying thank you and live in gratitude. Abundance is being grateful for all that you have and receive. If you want to shift your money flow, spend at least five minutes every day telling God all the things that you are grateful for. Another step that you can take to change your money flow is to change your beliefs and thoughts about money.

Let's explore some common limiting beliefs about money. As you read these limiting beliefs, ask yourself if one or more are beliefs that you hold. Why is this important? Because if you believe one of these statements, then you are blocking your money flow, blocking your blessings. And the belief *limits* your ability to attract and receive mo' money. How many of you believe any of the following limiting beliefs about money?

1. You have to sell out or give up your integrity to have money.
2. You have to work hard to make money or struggle to keep it.
3. You have to be lucky; you either got it or you don't; it is outside of your control.
4. It's not spiritual to want to have money.

Now that you have had an opportunity to think about these limiting beliefs about money, have you realized that they are not true and don't make any sense? I want to discuss "it's not spiritual to want to have money." I see myself as very spiritual, so once upon a time I believed that I had to suffer and be poor to be close to God. That particular belief was instilled in me through my primitive Baptist upbringing. Then I thought about my granddad who was a preacher. He had diamond rings, hundred-dollar shoes and suits, and drove a new Cadillac every few years. The hardworking church members made sure that he had what he needed and wanted. With those facts, I had to reevaluate my belief. If my granddad was religious and abundant, then my belief was false. Another false belief is that you have to work hard to be wealthy. Blacks, Mexican Americans, and poor whites are the hardiest working people that I know, and the majority of these groups aren't wealthy. That belief is not true. From my experience, I know better. As a child, my mama worked three to four jobs 365 days a year. We had food to eat, clothes, and a roof over our heads. Although my mama was able to get us off of welfare, we weren't wealthy. Having money is spiritual and living an abundant life shows how wonderful God is. You don't have to work hard to make money. And you don't have to give up your integrity to have money. I thought that I had to choose, my integrity or money. Of course, I would choose my integrity. I didn't want to be rich because I didn't want to be one of those so-called greedy rich people. There are many people who are wealthy, and they didn't give up their integrity to have money. Just think about it. I was attached to these beliefs too, but I saw the falsity in them and had to reevaluate why I felt comfortable hanging on to something that wasn't true. I realized that holding on to limiting beliefs makes you feel a little superior in that you can say, "I am better than you because I choose God over money." That superior-and-inferior mind game is your ego jacking with you. Keep in mind that money doesn't have arms, legs, eyes, guns, feelings, or thoughts. Money is not evil. Some people just use their money to behave unlovingly. We, people, project our thoughts, feelings, and emotions onto money. The result can be lack or abundance.

Do you think that God loves you more than Bill Gates? Let's get real. God didn't wake up one morning and say, "Oh, that Bill Gates is evil so I'm going to continue to give him more money, and Tyffany Howard is black so I am going to make her struggle." No. That's not God. That is you believing someone's programming. Bill Gates, Oprah, Beyonce, and so many others are wealthy because they are not stuck hanging on to false beliefs about money. They know that the universe provides an unlimited stream of whatever we create with our minds.

God gave you the power to create what you want in this life. *You*, or rather your mind, tells you that you are poor, that money is scarce, and that you don't have it. When you think those thoughts, your mind doesn't know whether they are good or bad; the mind finds a way to give you what you think about. That is called "manifesting," or the law of attraction. You can attract wealth or you can attract lack. What you think about and give energy to will come to you. I choose what God wants for me and that, my friends, is abundance. What do you choose for yourself?

If you are ready to live an abundant life, then let's tap on. By now you are familiar and skilled at creating problem statements that are more personal and reflect your life circumstances. However, if you just want to roll with what I've put together, then check out these sample statements:

- Even though I am grateful for what I already have, I'm open and accept more money coming to me.
- Even though I have this belief that I can't love God and have money, I'm open to the possibility that I can love God and have money too.
- Even though I can't see how I can make more money, I choose joy and I'm willing to let God surprise me.

Tapping for Abundance

This is my favorite chapter. I get so excited about tapping for abundance. Although I can't always see where the money is coming from, I'm always willing to be surprised. That being said, let's tap three times on the karate chop point, "Even though I can't see how I can make more money, I choose joy and I'm willing to let God surprise me." Before you start tapping, measure your discomfort level. Then with some of that unspeakable joy, move right into the issue phrases.

eyebrow—I can't see how I can make more money
side of eye—I choose joy
under the eye—I'm willing to let God surprise me
under the nose—I can't see how I can make more money
chin—I choose joy
collarbone—I'm willing to let God surprise me
under the arm—I can't see how I can make more money
top of head—I choose joy

Something tells me that I should have Whitney Houston's "Joy" as my background music. You can stop at one round or continue tapping more rounds until your heart is filled with joy in your soul. Don't forget to breathe and drink some water. Now is a great time to remeasure your discomfort level. Guess what? African Americans have officially tapped that!

We Out

We have come to the end of Sunday morning service, and I hope that you have read something that will inspire you to transform your life. People become so self-absorbed and immune to the pain and suffering of others. In writing this book, I wanted to bring awareness to issues that many African Americans experience on a daily basis. Moreover, I wanted to share this great tapping tool with African Americans. You can't change the color of your skin, and even if you could, it wouldn't change the fact that it's only skin. The point is that you are greater than the skin whose purpose is to cover bones and organs. Don't you get it? You are the divine being inside the skin, the body. I hope that I have made a loving contribution to this world. Our consciousness must be elevated. We think small when we live in terms of color, race, neighborhood, status, and yes, hair. The days of "I" are being replaced by "we." We are gifted and great people, so it's time that we come out of darkness into the light.

It wasn't my intention to offend or embarrass anyone. If you have been offended or embarrassed or angered by my words, ask yourself why. They are just words. My intent was to be honest, playful, and loving and act as a catalyst to awaken all of those who are still asleep. We do the best that we can with our level of consciousness; however, that doesn't mean that we aren't responsible for our actions. You are responsible for your life and for the lives of your children. Our ancestors were dignified, proud, and graceful. It is because of their ingenuity, self-sacrifice, and courage that you are free from physical bondage. Now, you enslave yourselves and allow others to enslave your mind. Stop volunteering to be a slave!

Be in support of conscious evolution. Step out of your box of victimization and blaming others for what you won't do for yourself. If you want to hang on to your reasons for not evolving, then so be it. Don't expect the rest of the world to stay back there with you.

Through our trials and tribulations, African Americans have leaned on God, and yet our understanding and knowledge of God is minimal. Our small lizard minds can't comprehend the vastness and wonder of the higher intelligence that we call God. It's our arrogance that limits our ability to let God in and also confines God to our small, ignorant perspective. What is known about the source is that the source is unlimited and loves all its creations. Our minds bathe in those low-frequency thoughts, and so that is what you have created. No, I am not saying that other people and their mean-spiritedness do not have an effect on your circumstances. I am saying that your thoughts and beliefs contribute to your life experiences. You can only start with you because you have no control over anyone else.

To dream a new dream, you have to have new thoughts and different tools. If you are up for the creation of a new life, then be open, take risks, and explore without expectation. I am reminded of a sermon I heard many years ago. One Sunday, my sister Fatima, who lives in Houston, invited me to attend church with her. It is a prominent black church, but I don't remember the name. I do know that the great football star Warren Moon was a member. Anyway, the preacher was discussing relationships, and he began to talk to the women in the audience. The preacher said that relationships were like fishing. He said, "Women, you will continue to get the same man that you are complaining about if you continue to use the same bait. If you want a different man, then use different bait." I submit to you that you will create a different life when you have different thoughts and use different tools.

In regard to racism, all that ugliness directed at you isn't about you at all. It's about some small people who live in fear, don't love themselves, and are feeling unloved. You can't fly if you're carrying a bag full of resentment, anger, hate, and fear. I'm not saying forgiveness is easy, but it will free you. I have a little wooden box that I call my God box. Whenever I have a problem, I write God and surrender the problem to him. Then I put the letter in my God box and forget about it. It feels so wonderful to give that problem to God rather than handle it myself. Everybody pays for the harm he or she does to others. I know this might sound corny, but love is the answer. Forgive and love yourself and all living beings. Remember to treat people like you want to be treated.

Well, I am writing more than I wanted to write. I can't stand it when people go on and on. So I want to wrap this up quickly. Tapping is a great tool to use to reduce or relieve some of our emotional and physical pain. You can tap on almost any problem. If you are interested in increasing your knowledge of tapping and your tapping skills, check out my references. At this time, please bow your heads. God, thank you for our time together, and thank you for light and love and for creating us just the way we are. Until we all meet again, God's people say amen.

Acknowledgments

Thank you, Divine Spirit-Universe-God, ascended masters, ancestors, archangels, Archangel Michael, spirit guides, fairies, and animal spirits! I am so very grateful for all the blessings that you bestow on me each and every moment.

Mama, thank you for all the wonderful gifts you gave me ... strength, integrity, kindness, love, respect for myself, and most of all, a love of God.

Daddy, thank you for telling me that I am brilliant, planting the lawyer seed, and loving me as best you could.

Reshena and Fatima, my sisters, thank you for your love and support.

K.Y., my baby and beautiful partner in life, thank you for stretching me and rising in love with me. Thanks for the lessons in unconditional love and always demanding honesty. Because of you, I realize that all shiny pennies eventually tarnish.

Anthony, my honey and hierophant, thank you so much for helping me to remember the way. We shared Eckhart Tolle, Osho, The Course in Miracles, meditation, and spirituality together. Thank you for juicing for me, cooking me dinner, exercising with me, traveling the world with me, and being my number one supporter. It was an honor to be your wife.

Catherine (catherinefergusonphotography.zenfolio. com), thank you for the awesome author's photo. Most of all, thanks for honoring our past life contract. We were like two little girls playing, laughing, sharing, and loving without a care in the world—that is, until reality came knocking on the door. All that you seek is already within you.

Dorothy and Michel, you are awesome friends. Thanks for encouraging me to finish this book and always having my back.

Nancy, my lucid healer (lucidhealing.com), thanks for being a mirror and, unbeknownst to you, helping me to see a healer from a true and real perspective.

Katherine Skaggs (katherineskaggs.com), my spiritual sister, thank you for the exceptional artwork for the book, for my wonderful soul portrait and for the healing you did on my heart.

Heather Neary, A Path to Gnosis (apathtognosis. com), thank you for the awesome Reiki sessions and for your support and assistance with my spiritual growth. I'm proud to be a member of gnosis tribe.

Louise Hay, thank you for the "I Can Do It" Conference in Austin, Texas, March 23–24, 2013. Doreen Virtue said to go home and, before going to bed, ask Archangel Michael to tell you what your life's purpose is. I did, and Archangel Michael spoke to me.

Thank you, Genia, Susan, Jerry, and Sedona Mago Retreat for saving my life and teaching me meridian tapping and Tao Life Practice. I am forever in your debt. Namaste.

Kay Christopher (eft–austin.com), my exceptionally gifted, beautifully creative, and sincerely committed EFT trainer, thank you for your compassion, kindness and ethic of high standards. You are an EFT angel.

To all my teachers in this lifetime who are too numerous to mention, thank you.

I love you all!

Check This Out

Resources/Endnotes

[1] Ortner, Nick. *The Tapping Solution*. Hay House, Inc., 2013.

[2] Craig, Gary. *The EFT Manual*. Energy Psychology Press, 2010, 2011.

[3] *The Willie Lynch Letter and The Making of A Slave*. Lushena Books, Inc., 1999, 2007.

[4] Id.

[5] Mandino, Og. *The Greatest Miracle in the World*. A Bantam Book, 1975.

[6] The Holy Bible/Maps, Books of the Old and New Testaments.

[7] Canfield, Jack, and Pamela Bruner. *Tapping Into Ultimate Success*. Hay House, Inc., 2012.

This Is How I Roll

Tyffany Howard, JD, follows her heart in life and in love. Inspiring clients, family and friends through her coaching motto, LIVE EXTRAORDINARY!, Tyffany lives the example of all she knows: LIVE EXTRAORDINARY.

Born and reared in Austin, Texas, Tyffany's love of learning earned her a bachelor's degree in communication arts and sciences from the University of Southern California in Los Angeles, followed by a master's degree in international relations from the University of San Diego. After a freezing cold winter at William Mitchell College of Law in St. Paul, MN, Tyffany returned to Texas, completing her law studies at the University of Houston Law Center, graduating in 1997 with a Doctorate of Jurisprudence.

Ordinarily, one would go straight into the practice of law. Tyffany, instead, devoted herself to realizing her childhood dream: to be a "movie star." She studied acting, and after extra roles in several well-known movies, and a cable series, she decided she had avoided practicing law long enough.

She served as a prosecutor in various Texas counties, as well as a Deputy City Attorney in Temple, TX. Always believing she could do anything her mind conceived, she ran for Bell County, Texas Judge -- campaigning as a Democrat in a majority Republican community. Tyffany knew that the loss of the election was a true blessing and the Divine Spirit expressing its infinite love for her. She recognized that the next LIVE EXTRAORDINARY discovery was emerging.

As she models LIVE EXTRAORDINARY, she discovered her true joy is being a motivational speaker. From commencement speeches to D.A.R.E. graduates, to the NAACP Senior Banquet guests with her inspiring speech, "God's Greatest Miracle," she motivates, inspires and uplifts others.

If you would like to be motivated, inspired and uplifted, please email Tyffany at tyffany@healingpathways.us or visit her website at www.healingpathways.us.